FACTORIES AND MILLS 350×120 FEET.

WORLD'S INDUSTRIAL AND COTTON CENTENNIAL

EXPOSITION,
NEW ORLEANS, LA. U.S.A.

Department of Installation.

PLAN Nº 2

MAP OF THE

CITY OF NEW ORLEANS

SHOWING LOCATION OF EXPOSITION GROUNDS
AND APPROACHES THERETO BY LAND & WATER

Sam⁰ Mullen
CHIEF OF DEPARTMENT

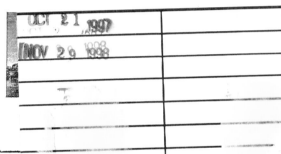

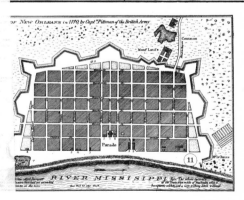

THE GROUND PLAN.

SCALE 1430 FEET TO THE INCH.

Main Building.	E—Art Gallery.	I—Grand Fountain, eighty feet high.
U. S. and State Exhibits.	F—Factories and Mills.	J—Live Stock Arena and Quarters.
Horticultural Hall.	G—Live Stock Stables, etc.,	K—Saw Mills and Woodworking Machinery,
Mexican Buildings.	H—Furniture Pavilion.	L—Wharf, Mississippi River.

The grounds embrace the space of 247 acres, bounded on the north side by St. Charles Avenue, on the south by the Mississippi river. The buildings front east towards the main portion of the city. An electric railway encircles the grounds.

PLAN OF NEW ORLEANS in 1770 by Capt⁰ Pittman of the British Army.

RIVER MISSISSIPPI

VIEW OF NEW ORLEANS IN 1719.

The "quartiers des Bourgeois" (people's quarters) consisted of several clusters of small wooden buildings enclosed by levees, and for three months of the year usually, from the 25th of March until 4th of June these quarters were transformed into island by the overflow from the river. The drainage was effected though a canal dug in the rear.

of the American Antiquarian Society

New Orleans
and
Bayou Country

Photographs (1880-1910) by George François Mugnier

Mugnier Instantaneous TRIPLEX PORTRAIT. 12 & 14 EXCHANGE [

NEW ORLEANS

Edited and Introduced by Lester Burbank Bridaham

New Orleans and Bayou Country

Barre Publishers, Barre, Massachusetts

1972

contents

DEDICATION

To Elizabeth Williams Seavey, the granddaughter of George François Mugnier, who cooperated with me on the first showing of the photographs of her grandfather, exhibited in 1955 in the Cabildo, Louisiana State Museum, New Orleans. I gratefully acknowledge her generous assistance.

To all my dear friends in the Crescent City, too numerous to list here, who have helped me in many different ways.

To my wife, Dorothy O. Bridaham, who shared my discovery of the flavor of New Orleans, and who has helped me express it.

Lester Burbank Bridaham

Mugnier

"Landscape photographer, publisher of stereoscopic and graphoscopic views of Louisiana scenery, New Orleans vicinity."

"Special attention given to interiors, lawn and other groups, plantation groups. Instantaneous photographs taken of yachts, steamboats, horses, etc."

Introduction

LUCKILY FOR POSTERITY, in 1931, George François Mugnier (1855-1936) brought his photographic plates to the Louisiana State Museum for storage—his nephews had been smashing the glass negatives for the pleasure of it—and said, "I thought they would be interesting some day."

Even fuzzily-developed pictures of the turn of the century would be interesting. There is a deep curiosity in nearly everyone about how fellow human beings live in other places and times (we are, most of us, not like George Eliot's Luke: "There's fools enoo, an' rogues enoo, wi'out lookin' i' books for 'em''). Photographs of a past time are compelling because their record of the look and the flavor of a time and place are unduplicatable in verbal record. This century being the most documented and preserved of centuries, our interest is seldom excited by the photographs we see daily of our daily lives, but Mugnier's photographs excite us with their historical record the way Mathew Brady's do, and Dorothea Lange's and Walker Evans'. We are amazed at the look of dirt farm poverty that we thought we knew about; we are amazed again at the dream-like fancifulness of a Victorian room—again, after thinking we knew what one looked like.

Mugnier's photographs are not fuzzily developed; they are pictures of more than professional quality—pictures reflecting deep feeling for place, for unhurried stark composition. There is talented handling of pictorial elements, light and dark, line and plane, texture and background, and a felt sense of human beings living out their histories in a given place and time.

By 1884, Mugnier was skilled enough as a photographer to open a professional studio. The New Orleans *City Directory* carried his advertisement:

> "Landscape photographer, publisher of stereoscopic and graphoscopic views of Louisiana scenery, New Orleans vicinity. Special attention given to interiors, exteriors, lawn and other groups, plantation groups. Instantaneous photographs taken of yachts, steamboats, horses, etc."

And his trade card at the back of his photos read,

> "G. F. Mugnier.
> Portrait and landscape photographer
> 12 and 14 Exchange Place, near Canal St., New Orleans, La.
> Rembrandt and Van Dyke Portraits a Specialty
> —Life Size Photo Crayons $15
> COPYING AND ENLARGING OF ALL DESCRIPTIONS"

Setting up as a professional photographer, however, does not explain a person's gifts as a photographer of feeling and commitment. And since Mugnier seems not to have left written comment on his own seriousness, Dorothea Lange's thoughts can serve us instead as a description of the commitment of a documentary photographer:

> "Documentary photography records the social scene of our time . . . the manner in which (institutions) influence the behavior of human beings . . . methods of work and the dependence of workmen on each other and on their employers . . . Among the tools of social science . . . documentation by photograph now is assuming place . . ."

This statement, which introduced an exhibition of her work, goes on to describe how new technology both raises standards of living and creates unemployment, and changes the look of cities and countryside; it tells us that documentary photography captures these changes, which are visible in forms and in customs.

Lange, who died in 1965, had this poem by Francis Bacon tacked to her darkroom door:

> "The contemplation of things as they are
> Without error or confusion
> Without substitution or imposture
> Is in itself a nobler thing
> Than a whole harvest of invention."

Some documentary photographers seem inspired to do other than "record the social scene." Some, like Jacob Riis, recorded the suffering brought about by poverty in order to persuade the middle- and upper-classes to alleviate that suffering. Riis, a Danish immigrant and a police reporter in New York City, published his book, *How The Other Half Lives,* in 1890. Photographers like William H. Jackson and Herbert W. Gleason photographed the wondrous Western landscapes in an effort to promote the establishment of national parks. In England, photographers recorded the lives of the Manchester and London poor in an effort to promote reforms. Even without written testimony from Mugnier, it is clear from his range of subjects that his commitment to photography went far beyond the simply commercial practice of taking pictures only when paid to do so. If Mugnier had been only a commercial photographer, we would probably not have such a broad and cohesive portrait of his city, in his time, as we do.

We can imagine Mugnier taking his tripod and 8 × 10 view camera to his favorite spot on the levee, watching the loading of cotton on its way to England to be woven into cloth and the rolling of the hogsheads of sugar along the wharves. One wonders how many glass plates he could carry for his morning's task, and whether he had someone helping him, an apprentice, perhaps. First, he had to set up his tripod, then get the camera focused on the subject he wanted to record. If it was a group of people, he would probably leave the tripod and ask them to hold very still when he held up his hand—perhaps for the price of a few coins. His glass plate film was certainly slower than ours and he was using a smaller lens opening, so even in sunshine, exposure may have taken several seconds.

Photography had come a long way by the time Mugnier opened his studio. It had been discovered in the eighteenth century that silver chloride and silver nitrate were darkened by light, but not until the nineteenth century were photographic experiments done, and not until 1839 was hyposulfite used to fix a picture and make it permanent. Around this time, Daguerre experimented with silver-plated copper treated with iodine vapor and, after exposure, with mercury, but his sittings required several minutes and the sitter's face had to be powdered to brighten the light. What was needed was a method whereby chemicals did more of the work than light, thereby reducing exposure time. Fox Talbot initiated such findings in 1841, and also first used a negative, and in succeeding years many people experimented and published their findings. Thus, by 1884 and the opening of Mugnier's studio, the taking of good pictures was not difficult. Dry plates made it unnecessary to develop a photograph immediately after exposure, and by 1878 an exposure time of 1/25 second was possible. George Eastman developed the hand-held camera and roll film in the 1880's, but there was a loss of sensitivity in the results, so Mugnier stayed with his cumbersome equipment—tripod, glass plates, large camera. Mugnier was said to have been a friend of Eastman's; other than that rumor, there is no record of how immersed he was in the wider world of photography—which was possible by means of magazines—or whether he was isolated from other photographic influences. The painter Edgar Degas visited New Orleans, and was an avid amateur photographer, but there is no record of their meeting. During Mugnier's career, E. J. Muybridge and the painter Thomas Eakins did photographic studies of motion; Adam Clark Vroman photographed the Indians of the Southwest; Alfred Stieglitz and Edward Steichen began their work.

Family photographs, with Mugnier at upper right

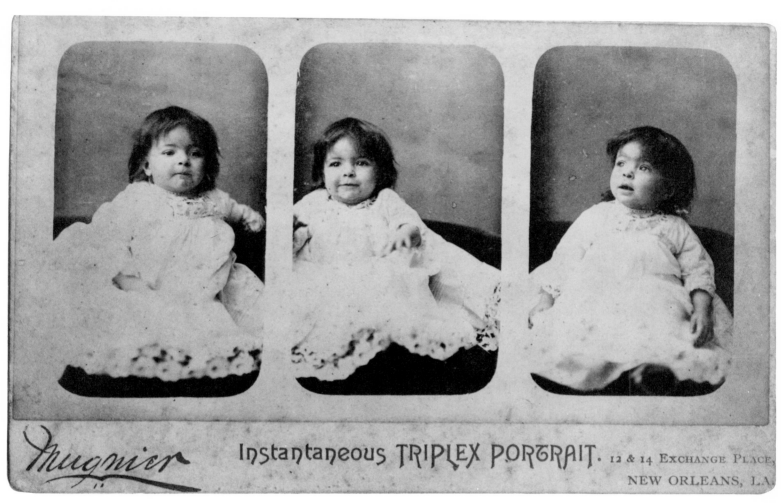

Instantaneous TRIPLEX PORTRAIT. 12 & 14 EXCHANGE PLACE, NEW ORLEANS, LA.

Mugnier's daughter

Mugnier was born in France in 1855, the son of a clockmaker who took him to Switzerland, to London, and then to New Orleans to live. The sea journey gave young George a life-long fondness for water and ships. It is said that George's father trained his son's powers of observation by showing him crowded shop windows and quizzing him on the objects when they got home. There is no record of where George Mugnier learned photography but there is no doubt that his fascination with delicate machinery can be traced to the watchmaking profession of his family. He liked to build or rebuild everything: clocks, cameras, and later radios and record-players. For a boat he owned in 1920, he made a rigging which allowed it to be steered from below deck. Mugnier was an engraver as well as a photographer, and was, in fact, foreman of the Photo Engraving Department of the *Times Democrat* in 1901. In 1920 he was a master mechanic at a shipyard owned by his son-in-law. (Mugnier married and had a son, who died young, and a daughter.) In 1885, Mugnier was awarded a bronze medal for photography by the Cotton Centennial Exposition. He was said to like properly brewed tea, to be a great talker, genial, and an opinionated man.

His photographs, spanning the 1880's, 1890's, and the first decade of the twentieth century, were not exhibited until after his death. The first exhibit was given in the Louisiana State Museum, in the Cabildo, in July, 1955, by Lester Brubank Bridaham, then Director of the Museum. The next exhibit was given in the 1960's by the Friends of the Cabildo. Many of Mugnier's subjects are only minimally identified because we do not have his own annotated prints, and the negatives were developed decades after the pictures were taken. But the photographs tell a story by themselves, so perhaps we do not need to know more.

I King Cotton

THE ORIGINS OF COTTON have never been precisely determined. It was probably used in India in 3,000 B.C., and for many centuries in the Western hemisphere as well—ancient Peruvian mummies were wrapped in cotton, and Columbus found cotton used when he arrived. The Industrial Revolution, and the resulting factory mass-production of cloth, made cotton one of the most important, economically, of all plants, yielding more cash annually than any other crop (although small cotton farms do not make much profit). It is said that before the cotton gin was invented in 1793, slavery was becoming unprofitable in the South, as in the North, and would have died out had not the cotton gin and the textile mills established cotton as the important crop of the South. (The planting of sugar cane in Louisiana also revived slavery.) Before 1793, the seed was removed and the cotton carded by hand. Cotton fiber clings so tightly to the seed that it took a person—usually a slave—one whole day to separate one pound of lint, while a gin can do it in a fraction of the time. Although the gin revolutionized the cotton industry, it did not remove the need for carefully hand-picked cotton because hand-picking could remove leaves, hulls, and dirt, and these accounted for part of the difference between low- and high-grade cotton. Even today, only three-fourths of the cotton crop is machine-harvested, because only gins with improved cleaners and extractors can produce high-grade cotton from mechanically-harvested cotton. Hand-pickers sometimes put the cotton in seven-foot long bags which are open at one end and looped over the shoulder. After the seed and lint are separated at the gin, the lint is pressed into 500-pound bales.

Despite the cotton crop returning much cash annually, it is difficult to earn a good living from cotton on a small farm. The return is small on a small crop, the soil must be well-cared for to keep producing, and the cotton harvest takes up only a part of the year. In the last two centuries, a small percentage of farmers became rich as cotton planters by buying very large plantations and using slave and low-paid labor. After the Civil War, many of the old plantations were broken up into tenant farms, but the sharecropper, although sure of some kind of crop and the security of some land, could seldom do well for himself, partly because of the poor return on a small crop, and partly because of the credit he was extended and then in debt for. Today there are more owner-operated farms than in Mugnier's time, but Louisiana has turned its economy largely to mining, and the center of cotton farming has shifted from the Old South to Texas.

The ante-bellum plantations were often based on sugar as well as cotton. The early Louisiana settlers had tried several crops, indigo, rice, tobacco, and even saffron, in a search for a staple crop. Sugar was introduced about 1750, failed at first, but then, after experimentation over many years, succeeded. Clearing the land was a costly job, and there were endless problems in ditching to drain the field, and in building levees to hold back water. By 1825, there were two hundred sugar plantations and Louisiana became known as "the sugar bowl." In the nineteenth century, processing was more mechanized with steam power and new machinery, such as the vacuum pan which pre-vented scorching, and the centrifugal machine which separated the molasses from the sugar crystals. Research was carried out on new kinds of cane to in-crease production and to withstand disease.

The plantations around New Orleans, built in French Colonial, Greek Revival, and other styles, were magnificent. In fact, one local sugar plantation owner, Valcour Aimé, was considered to be the wealthiest man in the South shortly before the Civil War. It is said that a planter needed $90,000 to equip a sugar plantation with machinery and slaves, besides needing a house, slave quarters, hospital, and jail. Aimé, whose plantation was called "Little Ver-sailles" (it burned in this century), also owned table service of gold (which he dumped into the river before the coming of Northern troops), an exotic garden with trees imported from other continents, a private railroad on his property, his own steamboat. Plantation houses often had many rooms — fifty, seventy-five — and dining rooms with fans suspended from the ceilings and operated by slaves.

Mugnier's photographs show us the process of cotton-growing — picking, hauling to the gin, baling, sampling, and loading the bales on steamships. He shows the workers and planters and where they each lived, and plantations in splendor and in decay.

Evan-Hall plantation

Plantation home

Carriage and riders

Out for a ride

de la Ronde plantation

Negro quarters, Belair plantation

Negro quarters, Belair plantation

Cotton picking

Hauling cotton to the gin

Cotton baskets

Returning from gin with bale

Cotton bales on wagon

Going to dinner

Cotton samples

Exterior of cotton pickery, New Orleans

Interior of cotton pickery, New Orleans

Loading cotton on river packets, New Orleans

Cotton samples on the river, New Orleans

Steamship loading cotton, New Orleans

River scene, New Orleans

Wharf scene, New Orleans

Weighing cotton bales

THE NEW ORLEANS CHAMBER OF COMMERCE describes the city as America's Most Interesting City; some claim it has enough culture, diversity, and tradition to rival New York and San Francisco. Many of its citizens maintain a sense of the past and of traditions, and value and preserve landmarks, so that many of the old sites which charm people today were preserved on film by Mugnier between 1880 and 1910.

After being Indian land for centuries, New Orleans was settled by the French in 1718. It was ruled by the Spanish from 1762-1803, when it was briefly held by the French again and then sold to the United States. Spanish architecture is preserved, as well as French, both of which Mugnier photographed. It was in the seat of the old Spanish government, the Cabildo—now a museum, that Mugnier's photographs received their two exhibitions. The Cabildo can be seen in one of Mugnier's photographs of Jackson Square. One of the French mansions he photographed, the haunted house on Hospital and Royal Streets, was ransacked by an angry mob when they learned that its beautiful owner, Madame Lalaurie, had been hideously torturing several slaves. The house was vacant for a long time, then rebuilt, and is now a rooming-house.

II New Orleans: City Places and Faces

Street names are flavorful, and tell of the past: Chippewa, Seminole, Cherokee and other streets honor Indian tribes; Ursulines, Assumption, St. Peter, St. Claude, etc., honor the Catholicism of the French and Spanish settlers; Calliope, Thalia, Socrates, and Homer reflect classical Greek remembrances; and thoughts and aspirations yielded street names such as Industry, Mystery, Pleasure, Virtue, and Desire (the last made famous by Tennessee Williams). Except in the French quarter, the Vieux Carré, the streets are difficult to find because they follow the bending and winding of the Mississippi River. Because the points of the compass cannot be used to travel the streets by, directions are given as "up River" or "down River."

People who live in a climate with a very heavy rainfall, resulting at times in 90% humidity at 90 degrees Farenheit, cannot escape the effects of the weather. Even in the middle of the night, a wall of humidity can be felt. On some days in July, New Orleans has a rainfall of perhaps ten inches. During a year, the city gets 55-60 inches of precipitation (about five feet); this compares with 28-32 inches for Illinois. The rain comes in concentrated showers with a heavy runoff and later, perhaps, long periods of drought. Microorganisms flourish and intestinal diseases proliferate. The climate slows down the tempo of living; things decay and rust and tumble down. The humidity intensifies the city's smells from jasmine and tea olive, roasting coffee, from the sugar refinery, and from the two breweries in the French Quarter.

It used to be even more a city of sound in Mugnier's day than today. There were riverboat whistles, street cries of the clothes pole vendor (whom Mugnier photographed), the charcoal man, the canteloup man, the watermelon man, the chimney sweep; the Blacks sang worksongs and shouts.

In 1812 the first steamboat arrived in New Orleans from Pittsburgh. The number of boats rapidly increased and the fastest steamboat became the biggest money-maker. In 1884, it is said, the *J. M. White II* made her maiden voyage from New Orleans to St. Louis in three days, three hours, and nine minutes, breaking all records. Her speed was never exceeded. The most famous race of all was between the *Natchez* and the *Robert E. Lee,* both of which can be seen in a photograph by Mugnier. The race took place on June 30, 1870, with crowds of people watching from the shores of every city and town, and proceedings cabled to newspapers at every telegraph station. It is claimed that more than a million dollars were bet on the race (and won by the supporters of the *Lee*). Many smaller boats also had races and sometimes, to gain speed, the safety valves were held down and often the boiler exploded; besides, there was always a danger of getting caught on a sand bar. Someone estimated that there were 5,000 boats lying at the bottom of the river between St. Louis and Cairo, Illinois.

The activities of a Black riverboat crew who sang as they fed wood to the boiler fires, were colorfully described by a European traveler as a fantastic sight, with black athletic bodies lit up by flames as they threw firewood into the fiery gulf and kept time with a hypnotic song. But the lot of the slave longshoreman was not romantic. He had to feed wood to the boilers and then, in any weather, after the heat of the engine room, go above and unload provisions and heavy hogsheads. Many longshoremen contracted pneumonia and died, or were killed by a rolling hogshead, or by an explosion. The white passengers, on the other hand, if they were cabin passengers, were provided with upper-class fare. One sumptuous menu was turtle soup, several kinds of fish and meat, potatoes, hominy, and plantain, muffins and rolls, coconut pie, jellies and preserves, preserved bananas, oranges, grapes, several flavors of ice cream, java and mocha coffee, and wine. Deck passengers, however, were treated contemptuously and often had to bring their own food and bedding. Professional gamblers made a living from the cabin passengers. It was estimated that at a given time, 1500 gamblers were working the river.

The problem of getting the ship safely to its destination was the job of the pilot, who first learned the river as keel boatman, and later, as pilot, had great responsibilities and received high wages. He had to know the river completely, including the colors and patterns of the water, in all weathers and under all conditions, which perhaps required a photographic memory. The pilots were often eccentric: one walked the deck at times of stress, and was called the caged lion; another slept in a wigwam behind the pilot house; one had a map of the river woven into cloth for a suit. For a long time, only half as much merchandise went up river as floated down because the largest ships had difficulty passing over the sand bars at the mouth of the river. However, in 1879 this condition was corrected by the engineer James B. Eads, who had jetties built to block the sand and silt. New Orleans then became a major port.

Mugnier's photographs of the city cover the river and riverside, including the loading and unloading of the steamboats, and many varied structures from different parts of the city—slums and mansions and decaying mansions, the French market and the business streets, an office, a barbershop, a church, a saloon—and in many cases, those who peopled these streets and structures.

Old three-master being towed up river

Praline seller

Natchez, Garland *and* **Robert E. Lee**

Packets unloading

44   *Unloading cotton at night*

Levee river packets unloading sugar hogsheads

West End channel

Jackson Square and River

Jackson Square 47

River view

Mississippi flood

The Mint

The Custom House, Canal Street at corner of Decatur

The French Market

The French Market

The French Market

Camp Street, Newspaper Row

Canal Street

Canal Street

Building (not identified)

Residence, Garden district

Chalmette Lodge

Old houses, Ursuline Street

Old houses, Ursuline Street

Old House on Toulouse Street

Historic haunted house, Hospital and Royal Streets

Old houses, Hospital Street

Old house in French Quarter

Old houses on St. Ann Street

Pole-peddler

Four Negro boys

Metal casting

Negro home, New Orleans

Tujague restaurant

Insurance and real estate office

Barber shop

Saloon

St. John's Church

Father Rouguette's Chapel

III New Orleans: City Pleasures and Privacies

NEW ORLEANS, IN LATIN TRADITION, manifests both religious and sensual fervors. Its churches are numerous; so are its nightclubs. Its restaurants are said to be among the best in the country and some of its bars are open any hour of the day or night, including Sunday.

Musical tradition in New Orleans is strong. It claims to have had performed both the first light opera and the first classical opera in the country. It has had three major folk music traditions, Cajun, Creole, and Black music of several sorts: spirituals, blues, sung sermons, work songs, field hollers, and shouts. Not long before 1900, the Black musicians learned to play orchestral instruments, and the first music by the jazz orchestras was blues, spirituals, and dance music from the French—quadrilles and polkas—which became ragtime. Certain musical elements kept from African tradition, flattened "blue notes," the stressing of weak beats, the repetition of rhythmic phrases, and other elements, produced jazz, of which New Orleans proudly claims to have been the birthplace. Basin Street was the home of jazz as well as famous brothels; Bourbon Street now houses the jazz clubs. A few of the many Orleanians of jazz are Louis Armstrong, Jelly Roll Morton, Sidney Bechet, and Fats Domino.

Along with its musical traditions, New Orleans has fostered a tradition of carnivals, the most famous of which is Mardi Gras, held on the Tuesday before Ash Wednesday. On Mardi Gras day, thousands of people mill about on the street, some masked, some in exotic or scanty costumes. It is an old tradition, and Mugnier photographed many Mardi Gras scenes, including the arrival of "Rex," the King of Misrule, the standard of one of the secret societies which participate in the festival. From 1830 to 1850, rowdy groups dominated Mardi Gras, throwing bags of flour at the onlookers and later, bags of lime. Fighting, drunkeness, and murder gave the masking and parades a bad name for a while.

Mugnier also photographed the Cotton Exposition of 1884-85, at which he won a prize. It was founded by an Act of Congress to commemorate the shipping of the first bale of cotton from South Carolina to a foreign port in 1784, to encourage the industrial rebuilding of New Orleans after its ravages in the Civil War, and to advertise the improvement of the port which allowed the city to become a major shipping center. The Exposition was held at Audubon Park, the site of two former plantations, and was a major World's Fair of its time. President Arthur opened the fair by pressing a button in Washington and turning on the extensive display of electric lights. The main building was the largest of its kind at that time, with a largely glass roof, covering thirty-three acres. The countries represented included Mexico, France, England, and Russia. There was a Government Building and a Horticultural Hall with hothouses displaying tropical fruits and flowers, including banana trees, which Mugnier photographed. The displays from different states included cotton exhibits, the Liberty Bell from Pennsylvania accompanied by a police guard, a Statue of Liberty

Denechaud's restaurant, West End

made of corn cobs and hay from Nebraska, and from Dakota, an Indian who sold photographs of himself, which were very popular.

Mugnier's photographs cover indoor and outdoor restaurants, parks and recreation spots, Mardi Gras and the Cotton Exposition. There is, unfortunately, no photographic record of Basin Street, or bars frequented by Blacks, or any of the less sedate bars or the brothels; there are, however, several fine Victorian interiors.

West End Pavillion

Dining Room

Saloon

Pool room

Modest living room

Elaborate living room

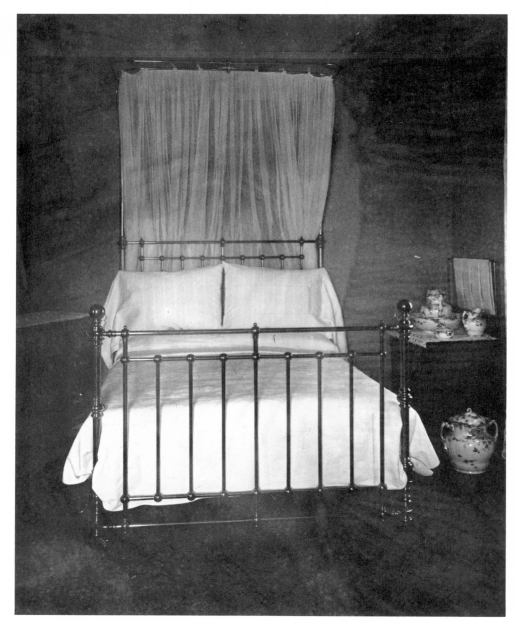

1885 bed showing mosquito bar

Bedroom with mosquito net on bed

Gate at old Spanish Fort

Alligators at Spanish Fort

Casino, Spanish Fort

Spanish Fort scene

Old submarine, Spanish Fort

Spanish Fort Opera House

*Construction of Fair buildings in 1885 for
Cotton Centennial Exposition,
Audubon Park*

Entrance to "Creation on the pike,"
Exposition, 1885, Audubon Park

Oak Grove, Audubon Park

View in City Park

91

Horticulture Hall, Audubon Park

Horticulture Hall interior

Banana trees in hot house

Cypress Arch

Mardi Gras scene, Canal Street

Arrival of "King Rex" at docks

New Louisiana Jockey Club

THE VAST AMOUNTS OF SILT carried down by the Mississippi River has raised the level of the river bed and the beds of joining rivers so that the rivers are higher than some of the backlands. To hold back the water and prevent flooding, miles of levees and a spillway must be kept in good condition, and pumping systems must pump out excess rainfall. (One of Mugnier's photographs shows the flooded yard of a New Orleans home.) There are also natural drains of overflow water, inland lakes, and bayous, which are the slow-moving inlets or outlets of the lakes and rivers. They are usually sluggish, marshy, and have dense surrounding growth. The word "bayou" comes either from the French word "boyau" meaning "narrow passage" or from the Choctaw word "bayuk" meaning "small stream." The discovery of deposits of salt, sulphur, natural gas, and petroleum, and the industrial expansion since the 1940's, have changed the look of the bayous and the lives of the inhabitants. These minerals now account for more than half of the wealth of the state, and make Louisiana the leading state in natural gas and oil reserves, but in Mugnier's time, the many families that lived in the bayou country all made a living from farming, hunting, fishing, and one-man industries, and in many places in the bayous the people still do. The swamp houses are sometimes built on piling and then anything, such as oyster shells, is used to make ground around the pilings. The houses, weatherworn and unornamented, are huddled in with the growing things so they have the appearance of being an outgrowth of their background. The cattle graze behind the house where the barn is located, and where the winter crops are stored. Chickens, as they peck beside the shallow water, have to watch out for crabs which might bite off a claw. There is always the battle with mosquitoes, snakes, and the water hyacinth, which was brought as a lovely new plant to the Cotton Exposition of 1884-85 and overran the state. People fish or hunt for the food the swamps and rivers provide: catfish, shrimp, crawfish, frogs, turtles, snakes. A famous Cajun meal is a well seasoned stew made with chunks of turtle meat and rice. Men and boys used to catch alligators with their bare hands. There are fur-bearing animals such as beaver, mink, raccoon, muskrat, otter, and the coypu or nutria, a beaver-like animal introduced from Argentina, all of whose pelts provide an income. One can still ride a pirogue—a dugout canoe—to the store across the bayou, and in certain areas the grocery boat, the *chalon,* comes by, getting through the shallow parts of the water with a push pole, using gasoline in the deeper parts.

In Mugnier's time, a man may also have had a contract with the railroad to make cross ties. He used a "bugboat" which can be reversed in rowing to go into the swamps backwards. After the trees were cut he floated them to a ridge and there removed the bark and squared them up with an adz. When he got a pile of ties, he took them to the landing where the railroad

IV Bayou and Back Country

Woodchopper

would pick them up.

Spanish moss is still collected from the trees and is used for stuffing furniture and automobile seats. Children in some of the bayous go to school in pirogues, and in the coldest weather, are wrapped in blankets for the trip. Religion sometimes comes by boat, also. One priest is said to have had two altars on his boat, one for Catholics and another for the Protestant services. Up and down the bayous, and the Delta at the mouth of the Mississippi, are people from many different countries who have struggled with the elements and battled with men for a foothold in the area. Every few miles another language is spoken. The most well-known of the bayous' inhabitants are the Cajuns, descendants of the Acadians who were expelled from Canada by the British in 1755, publicized in Longfellow's poem "Evangeline." Four thousand Acadians went to Louisiana in 1765; their descendants now number more than half a million. People often comment on the strong hold that the Cajun culture has on people newly arrived in the state to work in petroleum and other trades. Many newcomers like the Cajun culture — particularly its *joie de vivre* — and are soon absorbed by it, learning French, drinking black coffee, eating crawfish.

Two industries of the Delta are turpentine-making and cypress logging, both of which Mugnier photographed. Turpentine is taken from certain species of pines the way maple sugar is collected: an incision is made in the bark and the thick, gummy sap is collected in metal cups. The sap is boiled in a vat and the vapor passes into a pipe cooled with water. The condensed vapor, oil of turpentine, is stored in barrels coated inside with glue, to prevent the turpentine from oozing out. Cypress is a very important building material because it is light, durable, does not warp easily, even in flooded areas, and is resistant to rot. Getting logs out of the swamps has always been a problem because the trees in the swamp areas are in varying depths of water. When Mugnier photographed cypress logging in the bayous, the lumberjacks stood in the water or in boats or pirogues to saw the trees; today the trees are taken out by an overhead skidder, an apparatus of ropes and cables which drags the logs to firmer grounds.

Arcadian home

Country church

Tower and wooden house

Palmetto house

Log cabin

Bayou

Turpentine orchard

Turpentine still

Turpentine-making

Logging

Logging

Cypress logging in bayous

Cypress logging in bayous

V Cemeteries

MOST CEMETERIES do not command more than a quiet, contemplative passing glance, but those in New Orleans demand tours. In Metairie, for example, the cemetery primarily for the rich and where Mugnier is buried, some of the tombs are made from marble and granite and are designed like homes, with Greek Revival pillars and elaborate cornices. The cost of some of these is said to be many thousands of dollars. The reason for this fancy tradition, a European import, is that burials in New Orleans are traditionally done above ground, because the water table is so close to the surface that water fills up a grave as fast as it is dug. Cremation was not practiced because it was not accepted by Catholics. It is now possible to drain land and bury underground, but most Orleanians still do not. The poor people have been traditionally buried in honeycomb-like rows of plain vaults called "ovens," with no statuary.

Like the cemeteries, death itself has been traditionally dramatic in New Orleans. Not all of the old customs are still practiced, but many are, especially by the older generation. When someone dies, all the clocks in the home are stopped, and, like in Orthodox Jewish tradition, the mirrors are covered. Black crepe is hung at the front door. There is often a wake, at which the mourners repeat over and over the circumstances of the death, and then, amidst the food and drink and the visitors, they sometimes slip into a festive mood. Mass is said at the church, and then the casket is carried on shoulders to the grave, or drawn by horses. If they stop once on the way, it is believed another death will occur. Sometimes a band plays marching music. Remembrance of the dead takes several forms. Death notices often appear on the anniversaries of a death, sometimes with a poem and a picture of the deceased. And birthdays are remembered long after a person has died, e.g., "Aunt Jane would have been eighty-four today." There is still a yearly, city-wide expression of grief on All Saints Day, November 1. It is a city holiday, and much of the population visits the cemeteries.

St. Louis Cemeteries, Numbers 1 and 2, in the middle of the city, are the most historical, although not as splendid as Metairie. There are two graves said to be the burying-place of Marie Laveau, a part-white Voodoo Queen alive in Mugnier's time. One is a marked grave in St. Louis Number 1, and the second is an unmarked "oven" in St. Louis Number 2. At the latter grave can usually be found red cross marks on the concrete, even if it had been painted over the night before. The X and a prayer are said to bring a person's wish true. Also in the St. Louis cemeteries are memorials to the yellow fever victims of the epidemics of 1853, during which 11,000 people died, of 1878, and of 1905.

Mugnier took several photographs of the mausoleums in Metairie Cemetery and some in St. Louis, Chalmette, St. Rock, and St. Patrick, mostly of the tombs of the rich and middle-class. One photograph shows some plain brick vaults, and because two are open, reminds us that vaults were often used again and again, the old bones being pushed to the back to make room for a new body.

Metairie Cemetery

Chalmette Cemetery

120

Man with Skull

Vaults in Metairie Cemetery

St. Louis Cemetery

St. Louis Cemetery

St. Patrick Cemetery

St. Rock's Cemetery

126 *Metairie Cemetery*

Cemetery at Belair, La.